LOST & FOUND

IN THE MISSISSIPPI SOUND

ELI AND THE DOLPHINS OF HURRICANE KATRINA

LOST & FOUND

IN THE MISSISSIPPI SOUND

ELI AND THE DOLPHINS OF HURRICANE KATRINA

Katie Carpenter & Mary Carpenter

Tenley Circle Press, Ltd. | Washington, D.C.

CATALOGING IN PUBLICATION DATA

Lost and found in the Mississippi Sound: Eli and the dolphins of hurricane Katrina

Carpenter, Katie

Carpenter, Mary

ISBN: 978-0-9773536-5-1

Library of Congress Control Number: 2010935479

Tenley Circle Press, Ltd.

P.O. Box 5625, Friendship Station, Washington, D.C. 20016

www.tenleycirclepress.com

PHOTOS: Photos 1-15 have been excerpted from the documentary film, "Lost Dolphins of Katrina," produced and directed by Katie Carpenter and aired on the Discovery Kids Network. © 2005 Bahati Productions. Photo 16: © Katie Carpenter 2008.

BOOK DESIGN: J.A. Creative, Falls Church, VA

FONT: Myriad Pro, designed by Robert Slimbach and Carol Twombly

PRINTING & BINDING: Beacon Printing Company, Inc., Waldorf, MD, USA

For Dashiell, Revell, Oliver, and Edmund

ACKNOWLEDGMENTS

For their patience and wisdom, I am grateful to John Heminway, Josh Cook, Lisa Grossman, and Jonathan Lief, my co-producers on the film "Lost Dolphins of Katrina" and its companion Discovery special, "A Year On Earth." For their unwavering enthusiasm, I thank Diana Reiss, George Nicholson, Alex Meistrell and Ben Homer, and Marjorie Kaplan and Clark Bunting, who approved my first trip to Gulfport to film the dolphin rescue efforts for Discovery Kids Channel. And for their insight, dedication, and kindness, I thank the Institute for Marine Mammal Studies staff and trainers, especially Moby Solangi and Delphine Vanderpool. — K.C.

For their inspiration and encouragement, I am grateful to writing group members Natalie Wexler, Ellen Cassedy, Sara Taber, Jenny Brody, and Sally Steenland; also Sue Spock, Susan Land, Catherine Clifford, and Janet Bennett. For their close attention to detail, many thanks go to indexer Susan Fels, Rhoda Trooboff and Elizabeth Rosenbaum of Tenley Circle Press, and J.A. Creative's Anna Nazaretz Radjou. — M.C.

Above all, we salute those individuals and organizations worldwide who work tirelessly to support marine mammal conservation. — K.C. & M.C.

CONTENTS

CHAPTER ONE

Katrina Minus Seven: Introducing Eli

The dolphins at Gulfport's Marine Life Oceanarium seemed skittish during the last weekend of August 2005.

An aquarium with sea lions, seals, birds, and other sea life, the Oceanarium was an aging, turquoise, stadium-shaped structure that greeted travelers arriving in the sleepy town of Gulfport, Mississippi, its long beachfront lapped by the gentle Gulf of Mexico.

That weekend, the dolphins weren't performing their show moves as smoothly or afterwards circling their tanks as restfully as usual. Maybe they heard the hammering of plywood over the harbor-facing windows. Maybe they saw the trainers and other staff scurrying around to put the sea lions into crates. In the same way many animals respond to dramatic changes in weather, maybe the dolphins simply sensed trouble. Eli, the Oceanarium's youngest dolphin, had always been especially sensitive to changes in his trainers' stress levels.

There had been warning signs for days. National weather reports on Tuesday afternoon, August 23rd, described a tropical storm brewing in the Caribbean Sea. By Thursday the storm was reclassified as a Category 1 hurricane named Katrina, with winds up to 95 miles per hour. Katrina hit Florida's east coast, damaging homes and businesses, and killing 14 people. The hurricane next headed west across the Gulf of Mexico before turning north toward New Orleans, where the Mississippi River flows into the Gulf, and on to the Mississippi Gulf Coast.

"Spinning out across the Gulf of Mexico, it now looks like Hurricane Katrina might be paying South Mississippi a visit," cautioned the TV weatherman. Some residents of Gulfport, Mississippi, about 15 miles east of New Orleans, settled in on that hot Friday evening, while thousands of cars jammed surrounding highways with people evacuating coastal areas before the storm hit.

Eli's Birth

Four years earlier in 2001, Marci Romagnoli, her long silky hair wet from hours of training dolphins, stood at the window of the "fish house" on the ground floor of the Oceanarium. On that Monday morning, she placed her lunch order: "three pounds of capelin, two of herring, and throw in a little squid for a treat, please!"

As Marci waited for the dolphins' food, she spotted her friend Shannon Huyser, another dolphin trainer, whose dimpled smile lit up her face. "Hey Shannon, guess what?" Marci called out. "Our girl Jackie is in labor!"

As Marine Life's star performing bottlenose dolphin, Jackie could jump more than 14 feet out of the water. Marci and Shannon had worked long hours in and out of the dolphin tank over many years and grown attached to Jackie and her gang of dolphins. "Cool!" Shannon said, giving a thumbs up.

Marci headed upstairs carrying the buckets of fish. Through a small window in the azure blue tank, she spotted Jackie, her skin charcoal and her eyes deep and dark. Swimming behind Jackie came a tiny shadow – on closer inspection, a miniature dolphin covered with creases and wrinkles, and sporting fluffy whiskers that would soon fall out. This was Jackie's new baby.

"Ladies and Gentlemen, welcome to Marine Life's Main Tank," announced Tim Hoffland, the Oceanarium's chief trainer, at that day's show. In a voice rich with Southern charm, Tim continued: "You picked a very special day to visit us. Please welcome our newest addition, a dolphin with a very special birthday: today!"

A murmur of excitement went through the crowd. Jackie guided her new calf gently around the tank, maneuvering her large body to make it easier for him to nurse at her belly. She taught him to swim to the surface and breathe through his blowhole, which opened like a car's sunroof on top of his head to release a whoosh of air and sometimes a little watery spray.

Dolphins have fins like fish and live in the water. But dolphins are mammals. They breathe air through their lungs and are warm-blooded, with body temperatures that remain constant whether the surrounding water is warm or cool. Among dozens of marine dolphin species, the largest are the "killer whales" or orcas. But the most popular with people are the bottlenose dolphins, with their short beaks resembling happy smiles. In the Atlantic Ocean, bottlenose dolphins are the most common species, numbering about 20,000 in the Mississippi area and more than 200,000 altogether in the Gulf of Mexico.

Dolphins are considered to be among the most intelligent animals, along with chimpanzees and dogs. They appear curious about people and are friendly to them. They swim alongside ships and lead rescuers to injured divers and shipwrecked sailors. Swimming with dolphins has helped some people recover from medical conditions including chronic pain and anxiety.

But it was the dolphins themselves who were anxious that August weekend in 2005.

CHAPTER TWO.

Katrina Minus One:
Eli Joins the Grownups

On Sunday morning, August 28, 2005, Marci, Shannon, and Tim were called to a hurricane prep meeting. The Oceanarium's long-established hurricane action plan had to be flexible, because conditions often changed as a storm approached. From their open-air gallery, the trainers heard the wind roar with an ever-increasing pitch. Papers and equipment started blowing around.

Before dawn that morning, Katrina qualified as a Category 5 hurricane, the highest category, with winds at an alarming 175 mph and gusts up to 215 mph – more than twice the speed of the fastest baseball ever pitched. The New Orleans mayor issued a mandatory evacuation order for the city. "We're facing the storm most of us have feared," he said.

New Orleans residents unable or unwilling to leave sought refuge in the Louisiana Superdome, a huge sports stadium, where more than 20,000 people would remain for a week with dwindling supplies of food and water. The Red Cross began opening shelters in nearby Mississippi coastal counties. By Sunday afternoon, the National Hurricane Center described Katrina, one of the most powerful hurricanes ever to have formed in the Atlantic Ocean, as "potentially catastrophic." Alarming reports poured in from around the Gulf.

Dr. Moby Solangi, a biologist, and director and part owner of the Oceanarium, presided over the staff meeting. With dark hair and skin usually protected by a white sailor's hat against the harsh southern sun, Moby worked long hours caring for the Oceanarium's scientists and mammals, opening the aquarium early for school group visits, and crusading for the conservation of wild dolphins.

After the meeting, Tim and Marci nervously reviewed their lists:

Fresh water. Check.

Ice. Check.

Trucks rented and gas tanks filled. Check.

Medications. Check.

Extra fish. You bet.

Because the Oceanarium was located at the harbor's edge just a few feet from the Gulf waters, the trainers needed to be careful with their sensitive computer and medical equipment. To review what needed to be transported further inland, Shannon sat with Dr. Connie Clemons-Chevis, a local veterinarian who worked a second job at the Oceanarium. Dr. Connie, usually wearing a stethoscope around her neck, was a cheerful "dream vet" for the Oceanarium trainers. She stopped by at least once a day to check on her charges and also came on her days off to swim with the dolphins, often bringing her daughter Megan, a serious teenager who studied the dolphins closely.

Young Eli

Four years earlier when the time came to name the new calf, the trainers chose Elijah, making a trio of biblical names with Jonah and Noah, the Oceanarium's two other juveniles. As Eli grew quickly, the trainers were eager to start working with him.

But the decision was not up to them. Only Jackie and Eli could make that call. First Jackie had to be ready to return to work, leaving Eli in the care of the "Aunties," female dolphins that look after another dolphin's calf. And Eli, who spent most of his early months swimming tucked against Jackie's belly, had to become completely independent of his mother. For his first steps, so to speak, Eli followed Jonah and Noah to the "baby dock," where Marci and the other trainers fed them dinner from the fish bucket.

Young dolphins nurse from their mothers for up to two years, rarely eating fish before four or five months because their mothers' milk provides plenty of nourishment. But Eli started early. When he gulped down his first fish at three months, Marci rewarded him with appreciative pats and whistles to say "Well done!" When Eli circled back for more fish, she knew he was ready for school. At this point, a dolphin learns that fish come from individual trainers – not from the sky – and can start to form relationships.

Call it kindergarten for dolphins. First, Eli had to be taught basic behaviors that helped him make it through class and to follow commands like "come over here!" or "pay attention!" Trainers start by teaching the command "target," which means "touch my hands." When a dolphin does that correctly, he gets a fish along with the trainer's shrill whistle blow. "For about a week, it's just fish and blow, fish and blow," said Marci.

When juveniles get a little out of hand, as Eli sometimes did, the trainers teach the most important lesson of all, a crucial command that must be learned by youngsters everywhere: "Settle down." That's usually followed by "or else you'll be taking a time out!" at the side of the tank, away from the fun and rewards of fish and loving hugs.

Eli learned quickly. Like his mom Jackie, Eli had high energy and enthusiasm. But he was also curious, mischievous, and a little spacey. Compared to the other dolphins, Eli became more disoriented when moved to a new tank, swimming fast around the edges for a longer time before calming down.

At school, Eli soon progressed to learning the front flip, the tail walk, and the tail dance. Bottlenose dolphins have torpedo-shaped bodies for speed swimming in the open ocean, using their paddle-shaped flippers. Dorsal fins on their backs provide balance that helps them slice through the water. And using their powerful tail fins called flukes, dolphins can jump and dance. They are natural acrobats.

After each successful new lesson, Marci and Shannon shouted their excitement: "You rock, Eli!" or "Great job, Eli! It's all about you! You're awesome!" Of dolphins' senses, hearing is the most acute, and their tiny ears are tuned to hear the high-pitched sounds of whistles and trainers' cheers.

"The sillier and goofier we can be, the happier the dolphins are," Marci said. Soon young dolphins care more about cheers and hugs than they do about the fish. Then, if a dolphin isn't feeling well and doesn't care about eating, it still wants to work for the trainer. Dolphins love attention, toys, and anything that feels good on their skin. They like being rubbed. And they adore ice cubes, that nice cold feeling on their tongues, just as humans adore ice cream.

Soon Eli graduated to being part of the Oceanarium's 20-minute show. Each dolphin performed first alone and then in synchronized movements with the others, showing off tail walks and dances, somersaults and jumps through hoops. At the end of each show, Tim climbed to the high diving board and called, "Jackie, come to Daddy." Jackie did her beautiful 14-foot high jump for the crowd. All the dolphins wrapped up with a group "bow" – jumping above the water in unison, bowing their heads, and then performing a tail walk across the water's surface.

Dolphins communicate among themselves by slapping their tail fins on the water's surface and by a series of whistles and clicks called phonations. Clicking in rapid sequence, like the sound of a woodpecker pecking very fast, is also the sound dolphins make to locate objects underwater, similar to the orientation noises made by bats. The sounds bounce off objects and return as echoes, hence the term echolocation. By the loudness of echoes, the dolphins' natural sonar helps them to navigate and to determine the size, distance, and location of their prey. This sonar has qualified bottlenose dolphins for training by the US Navy to locate dangerous underwater mines, a threat to passing ships.

When the Oceanarium dolphins were excited about their work and about their human co-workers, they "came up screaming." That meant swimming quickly to the surface and popping their heads out of the water, whistling and clicking loudly as they came. Then the dolphins approached the trainers with their bellies turned up to invite a soft stomach rub.

Whenever Marci stepped out onto the tank's dock, the dolphins came up screaming to greet her. Marci usually hooted and hollered back at them, "Woohoo, yippee!" and "Hey y'all!" which they seemed to understand. The dolphins vocalized right back. This bond of trust and affection with their trainers served the Oceanarium dolphins well after Hurricane Katrina, when they needed to learn new life-saving behaviors under severe conditions – and fast.

CHAPTER THREE.
Have Mercy, Katrina: Jackie in Charge

As Katrina approached, dolphin rooming assignments were the luck of the draw. Jackie and the others already in the Main Tank could stay, because the steel-wrapped, wooden structure with 30-foot-high walls had withstood previous hurricanes, including the devastating Camille in 1969. Swimming around the Main Tank, Jackie seemed to know her job was to keep watch with one eye open.

Weather reports determined that the dolphins in the Bay Pool and Stadium Pool would need to be moved because both pools were closer to the ocean and had lower walls than the Main Tank. Moby began making calls. Two Gulfport hotels, the Best Western and the Holiday Inn, were several miles inland and had harbored Oceanarium animals during a previous hurricane scare.

"Sure, bring 'em on over here," urged the manager of Best Western's Seaway Inn. "You know we love having your dolphins visit our swimming pool, Moby. Don't you worry. If we've got ourselves a stormy weekend, then our guests won't miss swimming too much. Y'all come on down. We'll be waiting." At both hotels the pools were emptied and refilled with salt water to prepare for the dolphins' arrival.

Marci and Shannon knew the drill. As the wind continued to howl, they pulled on the sleek black wetsuits with blue or white stripes they always wore for dolphin work, climbed into each tank, and calmly approached the nervous dolphins. Moving dolphins is often a lengthy and complicated process because trainers must coax the 500-or-so-pound animals into sheet-like stretchers, lift them out of one pool, and lug them to the next pool or other destination.

Chief trainer Tim and his star jumper Jackie, both in their thirties, had been working together for nearly fifteen years – almost half their lives. They had an unusually trusting relationship. Once when Jackie had to be moved, as soon as Tim entered the water, Jackie swam straight into his arms without waiting for a signal. Tim was amazed by her display of faith and intuition. Now Marci and Shannon gently urged the dolphins into stretchers.

Plop! Splash! Over at the Best Western young Jonah rolled from his stretcher into the turquoise blue swimming pool with as much grace as could be expected from a 300-pound belly flop. The motel guests standing around the pool clapped and laughed with delight at the sight of three dolphins swimming laps in their temporary home. The manager was pleased. "Nice to have y'all back!" she exclaimed. "Now it's getting on dinner time. Let's all go in and see what's cookin'." The trainers were ready with coolers of fresh fish on ice for the dolphins, and the human guests headed into the dining room to eat and watch the Weather Channel.

The eight dolphins remaining at the Oceanarium included Eli and Noah with their mothers Jackie and Kelly, plus four older females who'd been moved in from the lower tanks to join them. Eli and Noah swam briskly around checking out their new tank-mates, who, the trainers figured, would quickly become Aunties to help babysit the young dolphins. Of the eight, Jackie seemed to move more purposefully around the tank while the others settled down to rest, swimming around and around in the dolphin version of sleeping.

After each Oceanarium show, once the last visitors trickled out, Jackie always took charge, circling the tank as if on a mission. One by one, she approached the toys – multi-colored balls, hoops, and rings – and one by one tossed them out of the tank with her snout. The younger dolphins got the message. Clean-up time meant bedtime was next. Gradually, they stopped horsing around and began swimming peacefully. Closing first one watchful eye, then the other, Jackie always kept a lookout when Eli and the other calves were resting. No one could have predicted how Jackie's vigilance over the younger dolphins would become crucial after Katrina struck.

Last-minute hurricane preparations were nearly complete. Some of the sea lions in crates had been loaded onto a truck and driven to Tim's house, where they were parked in his driveway for the storm. The rest were secured in pens at the Oceanarium. The maintenance staff battened down the remaining hatches and hunkered down for the night. Each trainer had a hurricane assignment, a place to spend the night at one of the hotels or at home before Katrina hit, so they could be on duty for one group of animals or another. The Gulfport mayor had ordered everyone to be indoors by 8:00 p.m. The trainers barely made it to their posts before curfew.

With no people remaining outdoors, an eerie silence hung over Gulfport as the wind picked up that evening. Eli and his dolphin pals rested in their watery beds. The Best Western's huge neon sign could be seen by the passengers in thousands of cars backed up for miles along the highway. Big red neon letters, flashing against a black background and constantly pummeled by wind and rain, read:

Stay Safe Everyone
Have Mercy Katrina

Oceanarium workers told CNN news, "We're merely hoping for the best." The next day, Marci, Jackie, and Eli got the worst.

CHAPTER FOUR.
Katrina's Storm Surge: Dolphins Under Siege

What really happened to the dolphins during Hurricane Katrina, no one will ever know. The Oceanarium trainers closest to the harbor that Monday morning tried to reconstruct the sequence of events. Some clues came from the chunks of concrete found inside the empty tank and the large metal beams hanging down like paper streamers from what remained of the roof. Hurricane winds had whipped the rising seas into a "storm surge," a dome of water pushed toward shore by high winds. So the trainers guessed the oversized waves must have poured over the high walls of the Main Tank and crumbled them. As the roof came crashing down, the dolphins spooked and ended up somewhere out at sea.

"Imagine being a kid home alone during a storm," said Moby later. "The house is shaking, the roof is quaking, the wind is howling, and the rain is pouring down. Suddenly you are picked up and turned upside down and next thing you know you are out in the dark, and the wild, all alone. Imagine that."

Little Eli had never been outside his calm, blue tank. He had never seen a shark, or most any other kind of animal. For that matter, he had never heard a boat, never learned to hunt for fish. At home, Marci was worried.

"Eli was the youngest, the most rambunctious, the least experienced. And no one had any idea where he was."

After pummeling New Orleans for hours early that Monday, Hurricane Katrina hit the Mississippi Gulf Coast with its strongest, right front quadrant aimed directly at the towns of Biloxi and Gulfport. Hurricane force winds blew for seven hours straight, spawning 11 tornadoes.

Because Katrina came ashore during the high tide, the storm surge pouring into Gulfport reached an astounding 30 feet, higher than a two-story building, flooding quaint streets and historic homes around the harbor and along the beach. Picture a solid wall of water 30 feet high and 1,000 feet wide – like a tsunami, folks said later. Literally tons of water slammed against the flat walls of houses and other buildings, destroying and washing away almost every structure within half a mile of the beach, and killing more than 200 people along the Mississippi Gulf Coast.

An offshore buoy measured 55-foot sea waves. The waves carried boats and debris hundreds of yards inland, along with pieces of offshore oil rigs and floating casinos that had been constructed on barges and anchored in the harbors. Appliances like dishwashers and refrigerators – floating because they are watertight – rammed into buildings and blocked the town streets. With its waves and winds, Katrina showed little mercy for the Gulfport Oceanarium, where eight dolphins swam nervously under a creaking metal roof.

These eight dolphins were hurled into an alien world of dark seas filled with sewage and debris. Above them were wrecked harbor containers, vehicles, pilings, trees, and building materials from tens of thousands of destroyed houses; below were sharks. Everything was entirely foreign. Imagine body-surfing through the undertow for hours in the dark, surrounded by boards, bricks, and broken glass. For these dolphins, who had never experienced threats or predators of any kind, the stress levels must have been sky high.

By that afternoon, Tim was able to maneuver his car around downed trees, flooded streets, and police barriers. He was the first to arrive at the Oceanarium. What he found broke his heart: a twisted tangle of painted concrete, metal, and glass; the roof blown down; the Main Tank empty. " The place was eerily quiet," Tim said. "There were no animals in the park at all – not one."

The trainers watching over the Oceanarium dolphins at the hotels saw water rising all over Gulfport. As the wind roared overhead and the rain hammered down on the surface of Jonah's pool, they looked at him speed-swimming nervously in circles. Dolphins care for family members and friends the way elephants and people do – very deeply. They worry when separated; and when the separation is long, they show signs of anxiety and stress. The trainers wondered if Jonah wondered: Where on earth could his little friend Eli be?

CHAPTER FIVE.
Katrina Plus One:
No Lights, No Phones, No Eli

Just after sunrise on Tuesday, Marci began praying for Eli's safety.

That was the moment when Gulfport's electricity went out. The hotel televisions could no longer provide hurricane updates. Next, the telephones went dead. The rest of the country knew that the Mississippi Coast was being hammered. The trainers at their windswept hotels could only watch the dolphins in the swimming pools and hope no sharp objects would land on them, as tree limbs, street signs, and metal roofing pieces flew around like confetti.

With phone and internet services down, Tim drove around town to survey the damage and check on colleagues and animals:

Best Western: trainers and pool dolphins, OK.

Holiday Inn: trainers and pool dolphins, OK.

Tim's driveway: sea lions, doing fine.

Shannon, Marci, Moby, and other staff: OK and accounted for.

The trainers were grateful to have their lives, although they knew major challenges faced them ahead. Moby set up a command post at the Best Western so the staff could communicate using walkie-talkies. It would be almost two weeks before telephones and cell phones were working again.

In the evening, the first missing Oceanarium animals, four sea lions, were located. Tim went out with crates to pick them up. Everyone was encouraged, but worried about the eight missing dolphins. At the best estimate, these dolphins could survive out of captivity for ten days. Having never foraged for their own food, they would have trouble finding something to eat. They would also be thirsty, because dolphins need fresh water, which they get from the fish they eat; drinking salt water will kill them, just as it does humans.

CHAPTER SIX.
Destruction in Katrina's Wake

After the storm subsided, all Gulf Coast rescue services were devoted to saving people. Later as resources became available, search and rescue operations for lost animals began. For the Oceanarium staff, first came the sea lions lost on land, because they were in more danger of dehydration or overheating and thereby dying than marine mammals lost at sea. In the harbor, Shannon saw floating refrigerators, truck tires, oil slicks – even frozen chickens that had spilled from a broken container. "It was pretty gross," she said, wrinkles appearing on her forehead. "I worried about the dolphins and all the marine creatures in that muck."

Katrina's aftermath was horrendous for every living creature. By dawn Wednesday, the winds had died and the waves flattened. News trickling in from around the region by radio and word of mouth revealed the momentous human tragedy. Communities all along the Gulf Coast had suffered staggering losses, most caused by the enormous storm surge that flooded six to twelve miles inland and covered almost every neighborhood along both the Mississippi and Alabama coasts. Hurricane Katrina killed almost 2,000 people in five states and became the most destructive and costliest natural disaster in U.S. history. The hurricane devastated about 90,000 square miles – more than half the size of California – and caused an estimated $200 billion in damage.

Meanwhile on national TV, the New Orleans mayor issued a "desperate SOS": Men, women, and children crowded for days in the Superdome and the Convention Center were running out of food and water. Lack of coordination and confusion prevented much of the attempted aid from reaching victims. Not until the next Sunday, almost a week after Katrina struck New Orleans, was everyone evacuated from the Superdome.

By the next week, while standing water in New Orleans was deemed contaminated by extremely dangerous *E. coli* bacteria, thousands of people remained stranded in hospitals, clinics, and at home, many stuck in attics or on rooftops. More than 45,000 Army and Air National Guard troops were summoned to help mount rescue operations and to guard ruined houses and businesses. In the Gulfport community, thousands of people were homeless, and many were still missing.

New Orleans and the Mississippi Gulf Coast would take years to recover. But for many people, following the story of the Katrina dolphins – who seemed defenseless and lost, not far from how they themselves felt – provided a welcome distraction from their own hardships and fears.

The Marine Life trainers were not the only ones worried about the dolphins and sea lions. In a crisis, marine biologists and trainers reach out from great distances to help colleagues in need. With Gulfport still in shock, two trucks driven all the way from Gulf World and

Gulfarium in Florida pulled up at the Best Western and the Holiday Inn. They brought critical supplies and transported Jonah and the other dolphins from hotel pools to safe havens. Folks from Florida's Sea World, ten hours away, drove all night to help with the sea lions, offering to take more than a dozen back to Orlando to rest and recover.

In Gulfport, reports of the Oceanarium's lost marine mammals began to spread. One sea lion was found lying on someone's front porch, another resting in the shade of a live oak tree. One was miles up the coast in a bayou; still another was stranded in the Lazy River water playground. A woman who found one sea lion under her SUV coaxed it into her child's paddling pool and fed it frozen fish from her freezer until a rescuer arrived.

Tim and the other trainers gathered up crates and organized helpers, including many sea-lion-loving neighbors and, when available, policemen, firemen, and Coast Guard search-and-rescue workers. The last surviving sea lion was found almost two weeks after the hurricane in a marsh thirty miles west of Gulfport, washed up on the street where Dr. Connie and her family lived. Of the Oceanarium's missing sea lions, almost all were saved.

One morning while rounding up the sea lions, the trainers and other rescue workers went to help a wild baby dolphin washed onshore and stranded in a deep puddle on a nearby golf course almost two miles inland, with no way to get back to sea. It took many hours to rescue that dolphin, because she was frightened and resisted efforts to catch her huge body up in the tarp and move her to safety.

Afterwards Marci looked out to sea where thousands of wild dolphins swam. From the harbor to the horizon she scanned the Gulf, looking for distant shapes above the water and keeping her hopes alive. Still none of her dolphins. Where could Eli be?

CHAPTER SEVEN.
Twelve Days Later: Lost Dolphins Found

"Guess what! We've got a boat full of gas for you right now, and we'll throw in a couple of biologists to help!" The phone call from Moby's friends at the National Marine Fisheries Service was exactly what he had been waiting for. Moby didn't know if the dolphins could possibly survive after twelve days in filthy water, dodging dishwashers and sharks, not knowing where they were or how to find fish to eat. But he wasn't going to give up now.

Earlier that morning, on that Saturday, September 10th, with sun streaming through his hotel window, Moby opened his eyes and thought about the hurricane as he had for the past twelve mornings since that horrible day. As the Oceanarium director, he was the one person most responsible for the dolphins' welfare. Moby focused his energies on one priority: finding the lost dolphins. He had spoken with friends at both the Fisheries Service and the County Sheriff's office who were managing recovery efforts and conducting offshore damage surveys. Every boat captain along the Mississippi coast knew that Moby and his trainers were looking for a very special group of dolphins. Around noon, Moby's phone rang. It was a friend who'd been watching the TV news. She wasn't sure, she said, but she thought she might have seen dolphins jumping in the background of an aerial shot of the Mississippi Sound. Something about their movement, and their way of orienting slightly toward the people on the beach, made her think they might not be wild dolphins.

Moby thanked her, hung up, and then paced around the room. Soon the phone rang again. For days Moby had been trying to arrange for a boat to take the trainers to search the Mississippi Sound. After his Fisheries Service friends had phoned with the good news, the next call came from folks at the Sheriff's office offering their helicopter. Then Moby gathered the trainers together. They agreed to split into teams: Tim and Shannon would head out on the boat, and Moby and Marci would go up in the chopper.

Marci climbed on board, and the helicopter whirred into the air. Adjusting her binoculars, she scanned the still, gray water. Within an hour, all the trainers were out watching every wave for fins and the familiar beaks, those "bottlenoses." Marci saw many of the Gulf's wild dolphins, but she was looking for her own eight Oceanarium friends.

Down in the boat, the trainers called it "Operation Bang and Blow." When they saw a group of dolphins, they would bang their buckets and blow their whistles. Wild dolphins would submerge and disappear. But what about Oceanarium dolphins? The trainers could only hope they might get a different response.

Not long after the helicopter climbed into the sky, Moby and Marci spotted a group of dolphins near the mouth of the harbor. They radioed down to the boat to check it out. Tim looked ahead and saw them. He remembers the moment with wonder – a flash, a glint of sunlight, a few clicks and squeaks, a shiver. All of a sudden, there were dolphin heads popping up all over just off the boat's bow. "Boop, boop, boop! They were all around!" Tim said later.

"There's Jackie!" he called to Shannon. "Look! There's Noah!" Then came five more, each of the missing Oceanarium dolphins recognizable by the size of its eyes, the length of its bottlenose and yes, the width of its smile. Jackie, all agreed, was simply beautiful. Then a pause, and one more little dolphin head popped to the surface, clearly the youngest one of all. "And…Yes!" Tim called. "There's Eli!"

"You rock, Eli!" Marci yelled her familiar praise on the walkie-talkie, so loud she hoped Eli could hear it over the noisy helicopter rotors.

Shannon was so excited she jumped right out of the boat and into the water with the dolphins – and floating rotten chicken parts and other junk. One after another, Tim handed her the fish stuffed with vitamins that they'd carefully prepared, and she started placing them in the dolphins' mouths, rubbing their bottlenose beaks and cooing to them with relief and exuberance.

Marci wanted to be in the water with the dolphins, too, but as she was more than a hundred feet up in the helicopter, Moby talked her out of jumping in. "Just wait until we land, Marci, please," pleaded Moby over the helicopter noise. "I've had enough excitement for one day!"

Excitement was everywhere. There was no mistaking how the dolphins and trainers felt. They all looked and sounded thrilled to see each other. You could hear the squeals of delight from the water and the crackling across walkie-talkies. "The dolphins were absolutely flipping," Moby said later. From chopper to boat to colleagues back on shore, the word was out: The lost dolphins were found! No one was ready yet to face the monumental task of getting these three-to-five-hundred-pound animals back to shore.

It was a joyful scene. The trainers in the ocean were feeding fish to the dolphins, stroking their heads, and hugging them. By now, the helicopter had landed and Marci had arrived by boat to swim alongside Eli. Shannon was treading water nose-to-nose with Kelly. Tim watched Jackie whistling and clicking away. The others in the boats were smiling and clapping their hands in recognition of this miraculous reunion.

Moby called Dr. Connie on the radio to relay the good news that the dolphins were found. "All eight?" she asked. "I can't believe it! All eight are there together? How could it be? That's amazing!"

The trainers were wondering, too. How did those eight dolphins stick together through almost two weeks of their frightening ordeal in the wild? Were they communicating with each other, guiding each other through the rough parts, cautioning each other to stay away from sharks? Did Jackie take charge of the group? Did she keep little Eli close? How could they all have survived?

These eight Oceanarium dolphins had never been housed together until the day before Katrina hit. But in the wild, bottlenose dolphins travel in small, stable groups of ten or so, called pods. Scientists who have observed dolphins' synchronized dives and made recordings of their vocalizations have a theory that wild dolphins remain in constant contact with each other while searching for food. By hunting cooperatively, they can cover wide areas and work together to surround schools of fish or trap them in shallow water. The Oceanarium trainers guessed that their Katrina dolphins had formed just such a natural pod.

But how and why did they end up in this particular stretch of water? Moby had a theory. The dolphins had probably been staying miles from shore, and then, as the water got cleaner and the debris started washing away, they headed toward the harbor. "They did exactly what I would have done," Moby said. "Wait out the storm with the Oceanarium pack and then try to find their way home." But did the Oceanarium dolphins have any idea where home was?

When Moby and the trainers finally calmed down, they saw that the dolphins were covered with scrapes and very skinny. Toni, one of the Aunties, had a big cut on the top of her dorsal fin. Jackie was the thinnest of them all. Tim's heart sank.

Jackie was no young dolphin. Tim was concerned about how she and the others could be gotten to safety or even onto a boat in the choppy waters of the Mississippi Sound. Moving such heavy, unwieldy, uncooperative animals is very difficult. He thought of all the times people had tried to help wild dolphins out at sea or washed up into rivers or shallow bays, and all the times these efforts had failed.

First things first: The dolphins needed immediate medical attention. Dr. Connie arrived by boat in a matter of minutes with her full medical kit. As she leaned over the side of the boat, rocking from side to side in the rough water, Dr. Connie realized right away how hard it would be to make the detailed observations required for a medical check-up. Trying to get a close look at her first patient was slippery work, like sipping hot chocolate on a roller coaster. But the trainers were persistent. Over and over, they brought the boat around. Over and over, they tried again.

Conducting medical exams on the rough seas would have been impossible if not for the amazing training of the Oceanarium dolphins. From an early age, they had been taught to do a "parallel station." In human terms, this is like backing a large car into a tight parking spot. As a trainer lay along the edge of the dock to demonstrate, the dolphin learned to pull up alongside. Now when Tim gave the signal, each dolphin pulled up alongside the boat, edging in close to give Dr. Connie access to its fins and blowhole. Her primary concern was infection in the open wounds, a particular risk in the Gulf of Mexico's dirty water, where contaminants from pollution and oil spills collected in filthy slicks, not to mention the car parts, chemicals, and sewage from the hurricane. Swimming and consuming fish that had been feeding in these waters would have made the dolphins vulnerable to all sorts of illnesses and infections.

Marci and Shannon were sure about one thing. With his mother Jackie weakened by hunger and wounds, little Eli was pretty lucky to have a bunch of Aunties along. As underwater nannies, the Aunties were capable of overcoming incredible odds and swimming through dangerous, junk-filled waters to guide their young charges out of harm's way.

The cuts and lacerations on some of the dolphins' bodies were serious. Tim wondered how the dolphins had spent the hurricane hours. If they had stayed in the tank while the waves washed over the top, had they been swimming around under the ruins of the fallen roof and girders? And after their tank became submerged, did they swim through downtown Gulfport with the overturned trucks, twisted signposts, traffic lights, and metal and concrete rubble until they were sucked out to sea?

At the end of the day, the trainers had to return to shore. They promised their dolphins to come back as soon as possible the next morning. Before leaving, Marci shouted out loud and clear: "We'll be back tomorrow. We promise! Stay safe, Eli."

CHAPTER EIGHT.
The Rescue Begins:
Come on, Jackie!

The weekend brought little time to sit around. The team had a major deep-sea rescue operation to run. On Saturday, Moby, Marci, Shannon, Tim, Dr. Connie, and the others gathered early on the dock to wait for the boat to take them out and to brainstorm about their approach. Squinting into the hot morning sun and trying not to breathe the stinky ocean smells, they asked each other: What are these dolphins good at? How can they help with their own rescue? Some can jump very high. Others can do fast tail spins. After a quick review of skills, the trainers realized that all the dolphins were good at "beaching" or hauling themselves out of the water onto flat poolside surfaces. But no dolphin can beach into a boat. They need something flat, smooth, and buoyant, like a floating mat. Where would they find floating mats? Call the Navy!

Finally cell phones worked. Moby made the call. The Navy Marine Mammal Program based in Gulfport had already brought portable pools with pumps and filters all the way from California. These were being readied to hold the rescued dolphins. A safe warehouse and men eager to help had come from local "Seabees," who earned their name by working as busily as bees performing construction for the Navy at sea. Trucks and stretchers had arrived from the Harbor Branch

Oceanographic Institute. Vets had come from the US Department of Agriculture along with boats, people, and other major resources from the National Marine Fisheries Service. All these were needed before the rescue could be attempted.

Now the Navy sent large floating mats, flat squares like king-size bed mattresses made of hard plastic. The rescue team got to work and linked four mats together into a makeshift platform that they attached to their Zodiac, the small, inflatable raft they used each day after their boat dropped them off near the dolphins. Wearing life jackets, the trainers climbed onto the mats.

First they wanted to spend time with the dolphins and get them comfortable with the mats and with their new training pool, the giant Mississippi Sound. Marci and the other trainers mimicked Oceanarium schedules by feeding the dolphins three times a day. They mimicked Oceanarium training sessions to remind the dolphins of what they'd learned, using bags of fish and whistles for reinforcement. The trainers worked from early in the morning until dusk to polish the dolphins' parallel station technique. In return, the dolphins got fish stuffed with vitamins and medication.

It was not easy. The seas were rough, and wild dolphins were circling just beyond the mats. They wanted the food, too, but were scared to come in close. Now and then sharks were sighted nearby, sending shudders down the spines of the trainers. They did not want their dolphins to get spooked, or worse.

By the end of the weekend, the trainers began to coach the Katrina dolphins on beaching skills using the platform. With a downward wave of his hand, Tim showed Jackie what he wanted her to do. Jackie came first because she appeared to be the weakest. She had been his star, and he wanted so much for her to succeed. Tim's hand swept backwards over the mat to show where he wanted her to land. He could tell she recognized the command. He knew she had the ability and the intention. But did she have the strength?

"Come on, Jackie girl. I know you can do it," Tim begged again and again. He realized that learning this skill could save her life. Finally, after hours of encouragement, with a tremendous splash and a belly flop, Jackie came up so fast and so far onto the mat, Shannon had to jump out of the way. Marci yelled with delight: "You're awesome, Jackie!"

Once Jackie was up, she got a fistful of fish to reward her and keep her spirits up through the day-long trauma of being moved. Now the trainers faced a second challenge: getting this 450-pound dolphin from the floating mat into the boat. It took six pairs of arms to lift the stretcher. Once on board, Jackie was held steady by caring hands as the boat raced into port. There she was moved onto a waiting truck. With a police escort, sirens blaring, the trainers drove Jackie through downtown Gulfport. They lifted her gently into the Holiday Inn swimming pool, where she stayed for several days until the Navy pools were ready.

Next came Toni. Hers was the same process but with more challenges, because her dorsal fin injury was deep. Gently yet quickly the trainers got her to the motel pool where she could rest and begin to heal.

Even as the hurricane death toll continued to mount, the successful rescue of these Katrina dolphins gave hope to Gulf coast survivors waiting to begin pulling their own lives back together. Local residents who had lost their homes were living in temporary housing all over Gulfport. Those camped out at the Holiday Inn were charmed by the unexpected treat of seeing these gentle animals, who had survived and were being successfully rescued. One resident said he'd lived his whole life on the Gulf Coast but had never seen a dolphin before. While waiting for housing assistance to get organized, the Katrina refugees enjoyed spending time by the dolphin pool.

After Jackie and Toni, the rescue team coaxed young Noah onto the mats and his mother Kelly soon after that, each chosen based on injuries and relative weakness. During the six days of the rescue operation, the Navy had finished setting up temporary accommodations on the base, and now the first four recovered dolphins moved into fresh, clean pools in an enormous warehouse. Navy kids shrieked with delight at their surprise houseguests.

Jackie's wounds were beginning to heal, and slowly she began to gain weight. But Marci wondered: How well did Jackie understand the risks still facing her frisky young calf Eli?

FIG. 1. Jackie with young Eli in the calm before Katrina.

FIG. 2. Before Katrina hit Gulfport, local hotels welcomed dolphins moved from the Oceanarium.

FIG. 3. Downtown Gulfport braced for the impending storm.

FIG. 4. Gulfport was smashed by Katrina's storm surge.

FIG. 5. The Marine Life Oceanarium was ruined by the 30-foot storm surge.

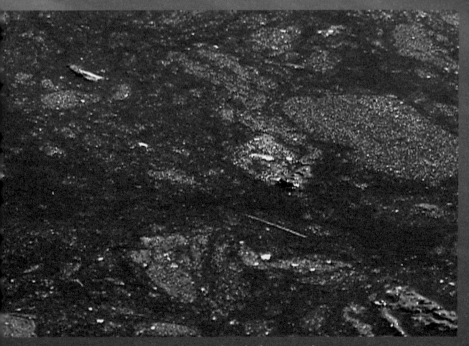

FIG. 6. Katrina washed chemical waste and toxic sludge into the Mississippi Sound.

FIG. 7. Searching the vast Mississippi Sound from air and sea for their lost dolphins, Oceanarium trainers spotted wild dolphins

FIG. 8. Trainers Shannon and Marci jumped into junk-filled waters to be with their long-lost dolphin friends.

FIG. 9. After weeks without food, the dolphins appeared eager to gulp down fish loaded with vitamins offered by their trainers.

FIG. 10. The Navy provided mats where the trainers cared for and coached the Katrina dolphins before their rescue.

FIG. 11. Oceanarium trainers found their last four lost dolphins just in time before the next hurricane hit.

FIG. 12. Of injuries to the lost Katrina dolphins, this dorsal fin laceration was the worst.

FIG. 13. Little Eli was the last of the Katrina dolphins to be rescued.

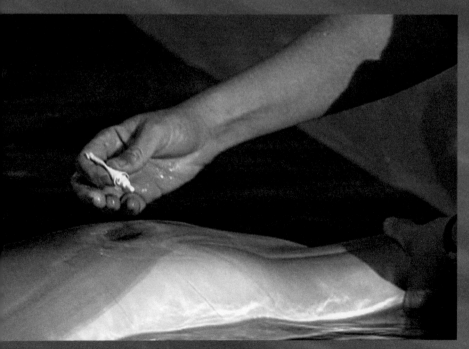

FIG. 14. At the Seabee Base, Dr. Connie applied antibiotics into a blowhole to treat infection.

FIG. 15. At the Seabee Base, Trainer Tim fed the dolphins.

FIG. 16. Eli is safe at the Atlantis resort on Paradise Island.

CHAPTER NINE.
Lost Again:
Eli and the Final Four

More than two weeks after Katrina, four of the Oceanarium dolphins were safely installed in the Navy pools, and four – including young Eli – were still swimming out in the Gulf. On that Friday morning, the trainers were up at dawn to complete the rescue operation. They had to hurry because another hurricane, Rita, was bearing down on them, now heading across Florida toward the Gulf of Mexico. If this storm was anything like Katrina, they'd have to pull the boats out of the water again and lay low. They needed to get the final four dolphins out fast.

With the sun beating down and the winds whipping up, the team sped out of the harbor toward the spot where they had rescued Kelly the afternoon before. As Marci tightened her life jacket and adjusted her goggles, she thought about young Eli. She imagined how afraid he might be with his mother and the other juvenile Noah already rescued and fewer of his caring Aunties around. His good friend Jonah, in the hotel pool group taken to Florida, had been gone for weeks now. Marci knew the trainers needed to reach Eli soon.

Arriving at the old location in the Mississippi Sound, they found a terrible surprise. The four remaining dolphins were nowhere to be found. They looked all around, banging and blowing in the worsening waves. They checked their GPS locators and scanned the seas. There was not a fin in sight. Had their dolphins been chased off by wild dolphins, Tim wondered, or something worse – by sharks? Or had they become disoriented in the rough seas that come before a hurricane? After many hours of searching, the trainers had to postpone the rescue. They returned home fearing the worst.

Though these four dolphins had by now consumed some food and vitamins, they were still very weak. The trainers were gravely worried about their littlest dolphin, Eli, out there lost at sea. Once again, Marci went to sleep praying that Eli was safe from sharks and other hazards until he could be found.

CHAPTER TEN

The Final Rescue: Safe and Sound!

For the next two days all the trainers worked from morning to night, desperately searching the coast with helicopters and boats for the four missing dolphins. With Hurricane Rita causing high winds, hope was running thin. On the third day, rescue boats were scanning the waters near Biloxi's Beau Rivage Casino, ten miles east of the previous operation, when Marci suddenly thought she glimpsed a little dolphin leaping into the air. She worried she might be seeing things. As her boat drew closer, sure enough, four dolphin heads emerged from the water: pop, pop, pop, pop. The trainers brought the boat around.

The littlest dolphin popped up and down, maybe trying to jump, but he was just too weak. It was Eli.

"Yay, Eli!" Marci yelled. "You rock, Eli! It's all about you!"

These four dolphins had spent more than three weeks at sea. Meanwhile weather services began issuing advisories for Hurricane Rita.

In the shallows offshore, the trainers lifted the dolphins one by one using stretchers and loving arms, working to get all four into the boats as fast as possible. As darkness fell, Eli was the last to be rescued, the hardest to catch, perhaps the most uneasy.

As it turned out, Eli had one more surprise for his trainers. In the truck on the way to the base, Tim felt a little spike protruding from Eli's forehead. He called for tweezers and pulled out what looked like a big splinter.

To Tim's astonishment, the barb was nearly an inch and a half long – the length of a birthday cake candle – from a stingray, a platter-shaped fish that hovers near the ocean floor. Everyone wondered about Eli finding himself nose to nose with a stingray: The curious young dolphin, probably looking for a snack, sees an unknown object floating near the bottom – does it look like a fish? Or maybe a Frisbee? Before Eli can sense danger and draw back, the stingray gets him almost between the eyes.

For many of the tens of thousands of people whose lives had been severely disrupted by Katrina and would remain so for months and even years afterwards, saving the final four Katrina dolphins brought joy in the midst of disaster. People watching the Katrina dolphins' rescue on TV had a rare glimmer of hope that their fortunes, too, might soon improve. Said the Fisheries Service director, "Amid all the destruction and loss from Hurricane Katrina, the dolphin rescue is a bit of good news."

On the way home, Tim and the other trainers marveled at the Katrina dolphins' incredible adventures, the amazing miracles of their survival, and the relief everyone felt to have them on shore and back together again. Marci could finally relax knowing Eli was safe at last.

CHAPTER ELEVEN.
The Dolphin Lost and Found

Inside the Naval warehouse, dolphins' clicks and children's giggles created a marvelous sound after weeks of tension and tragedy in Katrina's aftermath. One of the young Seabees, thrilled to meet these dolphins "up close and personal," made sure the kids on the Navy base got to see them as often as possible. And Tim proudly showed off his special group of lovable, smart dolphins to visitors from near and far.

Although the dolphins weren't able to share their stories, they contributed a few choice souvenirs from their adventure. In the Seabee pool, Tim began noticing unusual objects at the bottom. Jumping into the chilly water and feeling around, he discovered a wooden handle from a hammer, a pinecone, some wire, and a pair of men's underwear still wrapped in the store packaging.

Where had this debris come from? Tim explained: Just like Eli checking out the stingray, the dolphins didn't know what could or could not be eaten. They grabbed whatever floated by that resembled fish and popped it into their mouths. "They must have been really hungry," Tim said. "Imagine eating a hammer handle!" These items probably stayed in their stomachs for days before they were thrown back up. The Katrina dolphins' choice of food proved they could not have survived much longer in the wild.

Dr. Connie gave daily medical check-ups. With Gulf Coast schools closed for weeks after the hurricane, her daughter Megan often came by with her to help. Such good patients, the dolphins parallel-parked one by one in front of Dr. Connie and Megan and waited calmly for examinations of belly, blowhole, dorsal fin, and tail flukes.

Daily the dolphins gained weight and strength, and their symptoms of infection decreased. Toni's dorsal fin healed. Jackie put on weight and started to look like her old boisterous self. In the unfamiliar Navy pool, Eli and Noah at first stuck close together, swimming around and around with one's back against the other's belly as if they were attached – as if they couldn't believe their luck in swimming together again after the long ordeal. Gradually they grew more playful and better able to swim apart. Little Eli was growing fast; in a few years, he would be a big dolphin teenager.

As Moby later said, "If dolphins could talk, what a story these guys would tell. They would tell us how scary it was out there, and dirty. Thank heavens they were able to stay together. Now our burden is to look after these dolphins, and the wild dolphins, too."

All marine creatures now live in treacherous times, with warming oceans, oil and chemical spills, and other pressures on their survival. Connie's daughter Megan wants to become a marine biologist, because, she says, "Then I can look after all marine mammals. And the oceans, too." If Eli could understand her words, he would come up screaming with enthusiastic clicks and whistles and offer a courteous and grateful bow.

CHAPTER TWELVE.
Dolphins and the Gulf Coast Still Need Our Help

In the aftermath of Katrina, Gulfport was rebuilding, many local businesses were again up and running, and communities from Bay St. Louis to Pascagoula along the Mississippi Gulf Coast were getting back on their feet.

For several months after the hurricane, the eight Katrina dolphins remained in quarantine at the Seabee Base until they could be given a clean bill of health. Then all 14 of the original Oceanarium dolphins were sent to temporary homes around the country, as far north as Maryland and New Jersey. By January 2006 as the weather got colder, the dolphins were moved to the luxurious resort of Atlantis on Paradise Island in the Bahamas, nestled in the warm Caribbean Sea. After their harrowing adventure, a place called paradise seemed a suitable destination.

In the Atlantis lagoon, Eli and Noah, finally reunited with Jonah, couldn't stop swimming over, under and around each other, each bumping against his long-lost childhood buddies to make sure they were really all together. Moby was upset about the Oceanarium dolphins leaving the U.S. But Marine Life's co-owner David Lion argued that it would take years to build a new facility on the Gulf Coast, while "we have an immediate need – the health of these dolphins."

Returning the Katrina dolphins to captivity raised the question of ongoing opposition by animal rights organizations, such as People for the Ethical Treatment of Animals (PETA), to keeping dolphins in captivity and to dolphin research. Moby answers, "These are extraordinary animals. They have extraordinary capabilities. When they've been raised in captivity, we'd be remiss if we didn't use these capabilities to better our lives."

It was Moby's research on relationships between dolphin calves and their Aunties that helped explain how the younger dolphins survived Hurricane Katrina. The Oceanarium staff hopes that over the years, studies of the Katrina dolphins, after spending three weeks in the Mississippi Sound muck, will give a good picture of pollution's long-term effects. As for the larger questions about dolphins in captivity, Moby says, "Whatever you love, you want to protect. If we had not studied dolphins and learned about them, they would be dying in large numbers. Having some animals in human care allows us to save them in the wild."

Wild dolphins everywhere are in distress, and no one knows for sure the reasons why. Some possibilities include declining food sources and expanding "dead zones" – areas where pollution reduces oxygen in the water to such low levels that it's hard for most marine life to survive. As a result, wild dolphins are more vulnerable to a particularly vicious, rapidly-spreading virus that is thought to cause "beaching," when dolphins swim to shore and become stranded.

To those who chose to listen, the dolphins' plight during Hurricane Katrina made them messengers warning of a planet in trouble. Environmentalists blamed the hurricane's horrific destruction on global warming: Rising water temperatures in the Gulf of Mexico caused more overheated water to be sucked up into the hurricane's vortex, and rising Gulf water levels increased storm surge flooding. To make matters worse, in the fifty years before Katrina, human development and alteration of the Mississippi River's course had destroyed million of acres of marshes and wetlands, which had been fish nurseries and buffers for inland communities against storm surges.

The plight of the Katrina dolphins pointed out threats to other life forms, too – including people. Blame for the Hurricane Katrina disaster flew in all directions: at the New Orleans mayor for failing to evacuate the city earlier, at the U.S. Army Corps of Engineers for failing to construct better protective levees for that city, and at the federal government for failing to respond more quickly to the suffering of tens of thousands of people.

By paying close attention to what was happening with dolphins, Moby and his team could learn and take action. They have dedicated their lives to caring for these animals. As long as there's a dolphin in need, they will be standing by to help – on walkie-talkies, phones, boats, and planes. Inspired by the eight bravest Katrina dolphins – Eli and Noah, their mothers, and their Aunties – the trainers will carry on their good work as long as the Gulf Coast has dolphins. In other words, hopefully, forever.

Marci put it best: "I want to keep helping dolphins as long as I live."

EPILOGUE.

As of the fifth anniversary of Hurricane Katrina in 2010, the Oceanarium trainers and staff, based at Gulfport's Institute for Marine Mammal Studies (IMMS), were rebuilding and planning to continue dolphin education and conservation on the Gulf Coast for years to come. They were working to rescue and rehabilitate wild dolphins found injured or with serious infections.

By 2010, the Mississippi Delta wetlands were estimated to be losing about 24 square miles every year. Hurricanes Katrina and Rita had already taken large, hungry bites. Then starting in late April 2010, the same Gulf coastal areas were once again dramatically threatened, this time by the largest accidental oil spill ever, caused by a leaking offshore well that spewed more than 200 million gallons of crude into the Gulf of Mexico. Over some 100 days, the leak created an oil slick covering at least 2500 square miles.

While enormous efforts involving thousands of people and millions of dollars were still underway to repair the Katrina damages, oil-drilling operations more than two miles below the Gulf sea floor were not being sufficiently regulated. Even after the well was capped, this spill threatened not only Gulf ecosystems but also local commercial fishing industries that produced more shrimp and oysters than anywhere else in the world. In contrast to earlier oil spills, the leaking well leased by BP (formerly British Petroleum) created enormous undersea oil plumes at the critical season on the Gulf Coast for the hatching and rearing of endangered species, from pelicans to sea turtles. By late summer 2010, almost 5,000 birds as well as hundreds of sea turtles and dozens of marine mammals including dolphins had been killed by the oil.

While the original eight lost dolphins of Hurricane Katrina – Eli and Noah and their mothers and Aunties – were no longer on the Gulf Coast, they could have been smiling from afar on the work of their former trainers and the IMMS team, still saving dolphins at risk in the Mississippi Sound, still taking an active role in protecting this national treasure, the fragile ecosystems of the Mississippi Gulf Coast and the Gulf of Mexico.

FOR FURTHER READING

Non-Fiction

Carwardine, Mark. *Whales and Dolphins (Collins Wild Guide)*. Harper Paperbacks, 2006.
Introduces dozens of species of whale, dolphin, and porpoise, with information to help readers identify each species and learn more about them.

Howard, Carol J. *Dolphin Chronicles*. Random House, 1966.
In an adventure shared by scientists and two special dolphins, researchers study wild dolphins first in captivity and then after setting them free in their home waters.

Stewart, Brent et al. *National Audubon Society Guide to Marine Mammals of the World*. Knopf, 2002.
Authoritative information on all 120 species of the world's marine mammals, including whales, dolphins, and manatees. Over 850 illustrations, photographs, and maps.

Taylor, Scott. *Souls in the Sea: Dolphins, Whales, and Human Destiny*. North Atlantic Books, 2002.
At the Australia-based Cetacean Studies Institute, Taylor investigates the history, mythology, and science of dolphins, and finds they have self-awareness, compassion, and souls.

Walker, Sally M. *Dolphins*. Carolrhoda Books, 1999.
This introduction to dolphins describes their physical characteristics, life cycle, behavior, relations with humans, and threats to their survival.

Smolker, Rachel. *To Touch a Wild Dolphin*. Knopf Doubleday, 2002.
Learning to identify scores of individual dolphins, Smolker and her team find them to be more intelligent than previously thought, playful, and sometimes violent.

Fiction

Baglio, Ben M. *Into the Blue (and entire series, Dolphin Diaries)*. Scholastic, 2002.
Jody McGrath and her family are sailing around the world researching dolphins when a storm off the coast of Florida puts Jody's life in danger. A dolphin rescues her.

Hermes, Patricia. *Zeus and Roxanne*. Simon & Schuster Children's Publishing, 1996.
Roxanne, a lonely dolphin separated from her pod, meets Zeus, a troublemaking mutt, on a beach in the Florida Keys. They help three children merge two separate families.

O'Dell, Scott. *Island of the Blue Dolphins*. Houghton Mifflin, 1960.
Based on a true story, a young Indian girl is stranded and lives alone for years on an island off the California coast where blue dolphins swim, otters play, and sea birds fly.

INDEX

Katie Carpenter is an award-winning documentary film producer specializing in wildlife and the environment. She has made films about dolphins, orangutans, sea turtles, elephants, otters, sharks, and endangered species around the world for Discovery Disney Channel, Animal Planet, and PBS. Her documentary short, "The Lost Dolphins of Katrina," was broadcast on the Discovery Kids Channel. Katie is based in New York City.

Mary Carpenter worked for 30 years as a journalist writing about science and medicine for magazines and newspapers, including *TIME* and *The Washington Post*. She leads creative writing workshops and has written *Rescued by a Cow and a Squeeze*, a children's biography of Temple Grandin, whose knowledge of animal behavior has led to more humane treatment of livestock. Mary lives and works in Washington DC.

Mary Carpenter and Katie Carpenter are sisters.

J.A. Creative provides strategic marketing and creative services to businesses, non-profits, and associations. Based in Northern Virginia, J.A. Creative is owned by women who share a special interest in the environment.

Beacon Printing Company of Waldorf, Maryland, enforces a strict recycling program, is FSC (Forest Stewardship Council) certified, and uses paper from responsibly managed forests and other controlled sources. Beacon makes worker safety and health integral parts of its business plan. The inks used in printing this book are vegetable based, not made from petroleum products.

Tenley Circle Press, Ltd., is a Washington DC-based publishing house producing children's books with educational, ethical, and environmentally responsible themes. TCP authors, artists, editors, designers, printers, and marketing specialists share ideas and work together to produce smart, handsome books. TCP contributes a portion of sales income every year to children's literacy charities.